Thunderbird
and Lightning

Indian Life
in Northeastern
North America 1600-1900

Thunderbird and Lightning

J.C.H. King

Published for the
Trustees of the British Museum by
British Museum Publications Ltd

© 1982 The Trustees of the British Museum

Published by British Museum Publications Ltd,
46 Bloomsbury Street, London WC1B 3QQ

British Library Cataloguing in Publication Data
King, J.C.H.
    Thunderbird and Lightning: Indian life in
    northeastern North America 1600-1900.
    1. Indians of North America—Social life and
    customs
    I. Title
    970'.004'97   E78.E2
    ISBN 0-7141-1567-3

Designed by Harry Green

Set in Linotron Bembo
and printed in Great Britain by W.S. Cowell Ltd,
at the Butter market, Ipswich

Frontispiece Secoton. An Algonquian village of North Carolina
as depicted by John White in 1585.

Contents

Introduction

Northeastern North America is a huge and varied region, which may be divided topographically and ethnographically into four areas: in the centre are the Great Lakes, to the north are Subartic coniferous forests and tundra, and to the east the St Lawrence Valley and the Atlantic seaboard stretching between Newfoundland and North Carolina. The region was originally populated by many indigenous peoples, most of whom belonged to two language groups: the Algonquian and the Iroquoian, with a few Siouan-speaking peoples in the southwest of the area.

The virtual absence of important natural barriers in this region permitted not only the transference of ideas and the development of great aboriginal trade routes, but also the easy movement of population. This meant that peoples influenced and were influenced by each other so that cultural characteristics varied gradually over a huge area. While all tribes shared some traits, such as the method of farming among agricultural peoples, other characteristics might vary subtly from one tribe to the next.

The Algonquian-speaking peoples of the eastern Subarctic were nomadic big-game hunters. Their dependence on migratory game, particularly caribou and moose, did not permit large-scale political or social organisation. A tribe, loosely bound by ties of common identity and language, might consist of between fifty and a few thousand people inhabiting a large area defined by an important physical feature, such as a major river and its tributaries. For most of the year the largest social units were hunting bands, consisting of a few nuclear families related through kinship and marriage. At the time of seasonal concentrations of game, for instance during migration, numbers of hunting bands would come together to form a larger group for communal hunting.

To the south the Woodlands Indians exploited the specialised local food resources, such as wild rice and fish, in conjunction with slash and burn agriculture and the general hunting of animals such as deer. Settlements were larger and more permanent, and social and political organisations were more clearly defined. The Huron and Iroquois, the major Iroquoian-speaking peoples, possessed cohesive political systems based on the confederation of tribes or nations. These were in turn divided into clans, and a village, with a population of one or more clans, might have some thousands of inhabitants.

The League of the Iroquois, the most famous aboriginal political entity in North America, was formed in the sixteenth century by five tribes, the Seneca, Cayuga, Onondaga, Oneida, and Mohawk in upper New York state, as a response to depredations from Algonquian neighbours. In the eighteenth century it was joined by a sixth tribe, the Tuscarora. The League was founded by a prophet, Deganawida, in conjunction with Hiawatha, his follower, and regulated the external relations of the tribes and matters relating to the League as whole. Proposals were decided by consensus at each level of family, clan and nation before being put to the League, or alternatively, if they originated in the council of the League, they had to be accepted at each level in descending order.

The arrival of Europeans had a profound effect on Indian life and wrought radical and often devastating changes which altered the patterns of aboriginal society. The most important, and most immediate, changes which occurred were the introduction of diseases, such as measles, smallpox and venereal disease, which severely reduced populations. The most pervasive influences

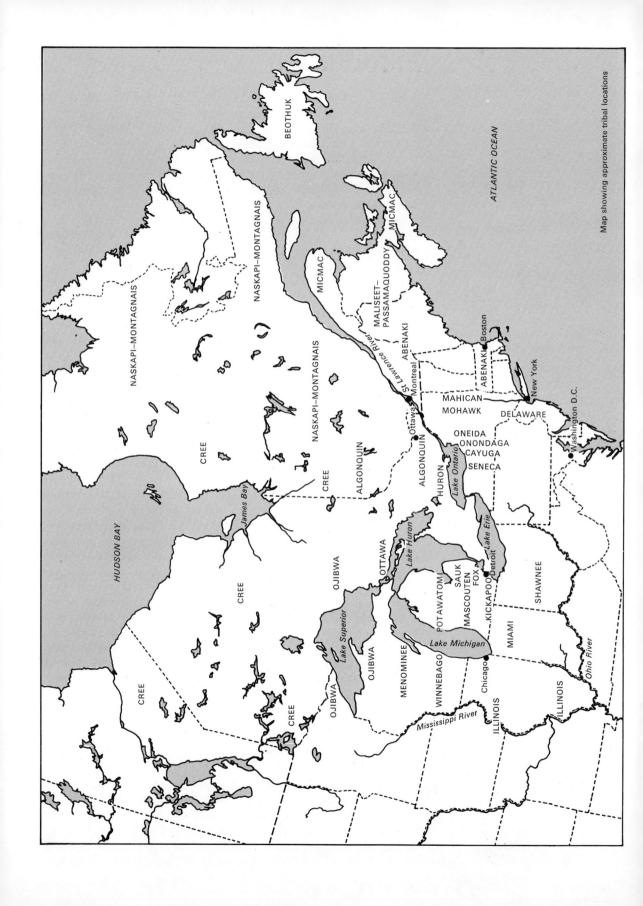

BEOTHUK

MICMAC

MICMAC

MALISEET–PASSAMAQUODDY

ABENAKI

NASKAPI–MONTAGNAIS

NASKAPI–MONTAGNAIS

NASKAPI–MONTAGNAIS

ATLANTIC OCEAN

Map showing approximate tribal locations

St Lawrence River

Montreal

ABENAKI

Boston

MAHICAN

MOHAWK

New York

DELAWARE

Washington D.C.

CREE

Ottawa

ALGONQUIN

ALGONQUIN

ONEIDA

ONONDAGA

CAYUGA

SENECA

CREE

HURON

Lake Ontario

HUDSON BAY

James Bay

Lake Erie

Lake Huron

CREE

OJIBWA

OTTAWA

Detroit

SAUK

FOX

POTAWATOMI

MASCOUTEN

KICKAPOO

SHAWNEE

CREE

Lake Superior

OJIBWA

MENOMINEE

WINNEBAGO

Lake Michigan

MIAMI

Chicago

CREE

OJIBWA

ILLINOIS

ILLINOIS

Mississippi River

Ohio River

were, however, probably those of the fur trade. French, Dutch, British and American traders and trading companies competed for access to Indian tribes willing and able to exchange furs for tools and utensils, and to provide food for traders in exchange for rum. The fur trade encouraged competition between individuals and households, communities and tribes, all of whom became increasingly dependent on the fur trade from the seventeenth century onwards. Perhaps the best-known example of fur trade rivalry is that between the Huron and Iroquois in the seventeenth century. A traditional feud between two peoples was exacerbated by the sudden growth in the fur trade and the decline in the availability of beaver in the traditional territories of the Iroquois, in what is now New York state. The Huron, in Ontario, were able to trade with tribes to their north and west whose territory was still rich in beaver. The Iroquois sought to gain access to this trade and, to achieve their ends, defeated and dispersed the Huron during the 1640s. At the same time as the fur trade altered the economic basis of interior tribes, other peoples on the coast were affected by European settlement, which in many areas in the eighteenth and nineteenth centuries followed on from the fur trade, and gradually outgrew it in importance.

This book, published in connection with an exhibition at the Museum of Mankind, provides an outline of Indian life in Northeastern North America from 1600 to 1900. The range it covers is extensive; the area is huge and the three centuries described, from the first sustained European presence in the seventeenth century, represents a period of highly complex cultural history of which only a few salient points may be mentioned here.

Presenting a picture of Woodlands culture on the basis of museum collections creates certain difficulties. The complex ethnography and history of the Northeast is reflected in the haphazard nature of museum collections from colonial North America. Most Woodlands artefacts in European collections were obtained between the mid-eighteenth and mid-nineteenth centuries by people such as administrators, soldiers, explorers and traders, all of whom were unlikely to record details of their collections. Very occasionally collectors were men of learning who obtained artefacts for educational purposes for Cabinets of Curiosities. Even then the vast majority of artefacts were acquired with little or no information as to who made them or which tribe they came from, presumably because, whatever the collector's reasons for obtaining artefacts, this was not the principle purpose of his stay in North America. We are usually lucky to know the name of the collector and the dates when he was in America. Artefacts obtained from Subartic peoples are on the whole better documented because they were obtained at a later date, occasionally by anthropologists, but more often by people, still traders or soldiers, who possessed a greater awareness than their predecessors of what they were doing.

A further problem is presented by the nature of the collections, which by no means represents the full range of material culture of the Woodlands Indians. This is partly because large artefacts such as canoes, and perishable material such as food, were not collected, but the principle reason is that collectors and museum curators in the eighteenth and nineteenth centuries seem to have been more interested in acquiring objects that were unusual, historic, difficult to obtain and apparently bizarre than more representative Indian artefacts. In Europe wampum belts, calumets and scalps were more highly appreciated than everyday clothing and items such as wood spoons and bowls, which may have been considered similar to forms still in use.

This bias obscures our understanding of ordinary material culture and, because of the lack of documentation of the 'exotic' artefacts, does not necessarily contribute to a greater appreciation of Indian symbolism, mythology and religion. It is, however, possible to understand how this distortion in favour of the unusual came about. A nineteenth-century explorer, for instance, travelling northwest from the Great Lakes towards the Arctic shore might seek to obtain artefacts from the farthest point of his travels which would then reflect his qualities as explorer; at the same time he might return with Indian clothing and equipment which had been used en route. The resultant collection might appear confusing 150 years later. Conversely, the trader, whether based in eastern Canada, New England or Europe, might try to obtain things which would be recognised by family and friends as of obviously Indian origin. These might be significant artefacts in their own right, such as masks or wampum belts, or they might be souvenir models, of wigwams or canoes, of little use to Indians. Soldiers, in the colonial wars of the eighteenth century were important collectors, given to fitting themselves out with Indian costumes; few of these costumes survive complete and for those that do we do not know whether the items were assembled from one tribe, or one person, and moreover we cannot assume that artefacts made for European use were of types also used by Indians. Another distortion in museum collections arises because of the apparent reluctance of collectors to obtain material showing evidence of European materials and ideas. The collections of the British Museum, for instance, include few examples of Woodlands silver ornaments because, of course, silver was made by French and British silversmiths for the Indian trade. Similarly, woven splint baskets were not brought to England, perhaps because they were unconsciously recognised as having a non-Indian origin.

The unstated, but very evident bias of collections towards the highly-beautified and unusual artefact of obviously Indian, and preferably aboriginal, design has contributed recently to an increasing interest in Indian art in museums. Because there is seldom any direct information about Indian aesthetics, and little about the roles of artists and craftsmen, Western appreciation of Indian art is often largely intuitive. It depends on understanding the extent of the craftsman's skill with his tools – here largely the crooked knife (24) and the awl and needle – and his awareness of the full potential of the materials available. In Woodlands art the preparation of skin was fundamental to the creation of embroidery, which in turn depended on a more variable knowledge of the fine uses to which moosehair and porcupine quills could be put. But perhaps the most important aspect of Western art appreciation of Indian artefacts is a comprehension, however rudimentary, of the cultural context and the traditional forms of artefacts and their use. If an appreciation of technique is combined with this then beautiful and significant artefacts, often of disparate origin, can be grouped together and understood for their emotional and symbolic content. In this way the general meaning of the material object can become the focus of attention, within the wider context of Woodlands culture. This is important because so few artefacts are documented, but it is also extremely unfortunate because many of the decorative elements of artefacts may relate to personal spirits, knowledge of which was gained by individuals in spirit quests and retained for personal use only. This means that individualistic artistic statements in whole media such as porcupine quillwork and moosehair embroidery are lost, and that one aspect of surviving artefacts is and will always be incomprehensible.

Many other identifiable ideas are expressed in Woodlands art, apart from the representation of guardian spirits. Clan symbols such as the turtle may be carved on Iroquois pipes (77), records may be made of individual achievements, in war for instance on clubs (90). The Iroquois False-Face society use masks in curing rituals whose context is well documented (59-62), and the Naskapi painted their caribou skin coats with representations of this animal, on which they depended for their survival (39). Wampum belts contained specific meanings in their geometric forms (72), while Mide scrolls covered with incised and painted figures recorded traditional narratives and songs (69). Important spirits such as Thunderbirds (65, 70, 71, 76) and Underwater Panthers (66) are depicted on bags and drums which may relate to the Midewiwin, a Great Lakes cult combining shamanism with a means of preserving traditional lore.

These Thunderbirds, or Thunderers, are of general importance in Algonquian and Iroquoian mythology as creatures of the Upper World associated with fertility and with the creation of clouds and rain. They are in constant state of warfare with the spirits of the Under World, against whom they use lightning. Although not the most important spirits, their distinctive abstract bird-form is easily recognised, and so can serve as a symbol for the poorly understood beauty of Woodlands artefacts.

1 Hunting and farming

Scarcely any device which the ingenuity of man has discovered for ensnaring or destroying those animals that supply them with food, or whose skins are valuable to Europeans, is unknown to them.
(Carver 283-4)

Hunting provided the major source of food for most peoples in the Northeast, although agriculture was more important among some tribes, particularly the Huron and the Iroquois. The most significant animals were deer, moose, bear and smaller mammals, and maize, beans and squash were the staple crops. The diet could be supplemented by gathering wild berries, maple syrup, wild rice (along waterways), by fishing, which was particularly important on the Great Lakes and on rivers, and by collecting shellfish (on the Atlantic coast).

The Iroquoian farming peoples lived in semi-permanent villages, which were moved every ten or twenty years as the soil nutrients in the fields and gardens became exhausted. It was the women who cultivated the fields, tended the crops, and prepared the food. Maize was eaten in many different ways – roasted, boiled, made into soups and bread, fried, or turned into pop-corn. It could also be mixed with beans, squash and pumpkin, boiled with meat, or turned into a pudding by adding maple syrup. During winter expeditions would be made from the village to gather wild crops and maple syrup, to fish and to hunt.

Among the peoples who lived purely by hunting, separate camps would be established during the winter and, though occasionally several bands might come together to hunt a large herd of caribou or exploit a large fish run, it was only in the summer that whole bands would gather. Hunting was a purely male activity among all tribes.

1. Indians fishing from a canoe; from a French manuscript known as the 'Codex Canadensis', *c*.1700.

La pesche des Sauuages p. 13
passinassionek Je decris cette pesche ailleur, qui est une des
choses tres merueilleusses touchand La F. 19 pesche.

kouabagan

atironek

Bareskoupan

eskan

Instrumens pour La pesche

2. Joe Pielpole, Passamaquoddy, fishing with a spear by the light of a birchbark torch, at Peter Dana Point Reservation, Maine, c.1910.

3. Early-nineteenth-century painting of Micmacs shooting geese. Outside the birchbark wigwam is a toboggan with a dead goose on it; more birds and animals hang from the sides of the wigwam. Inside, a woman is holding a baby in a cradle and beside her are several birchbark containers, three of which are of the kind decorated with porcupine quillwork often made for sale to whites.

4. Two Minnesota Ojibwa setting out to
hunt deer. They are both wearing a
mixture of skin and wool clothing,
typical of the last quarter of the
nineteenth century.

5. Cree bow and iron-tipped arrows
with skin bowcase, quiver and strap,
collected by Major George Seton at Fort
Garry, Winnipeg, 1858.

6. Nineteenth-century hunting equipment. *Left to right* (a) Delaware bow collected in Ontario (length 130 cm); (b) Micmac bow collected by T. G. B. Lloyd at Abraham Joe's wigwam, Grand Pond, Newfoundland in September 1873 (length 158 cm); (c) Algonquian or Athapaskan leister spear; the shaft is incomplete (length 128 cm); (d) Cree (?) bow and three arrows with smoked skin bowcase and quiver, both decorated with red cloth, white beads and quill-wrapped fringes (length of bow 130 cm).

BELOW
7. Knives and knife sheaths from the Great Lakes and northern Plains. *Left to right* (a) three skin sheaths decorated with quillwork in zig-zag line technique (lengths without straps 23, 23, 22 cm); (b) knife with bone or antler handle and skin sheath (length 43 cm); (c) knife with horn handle inlaid with bone and cartridge butts, with a skin sheath (length 38 cm); knife with bone or antler handle (length 36 cm).

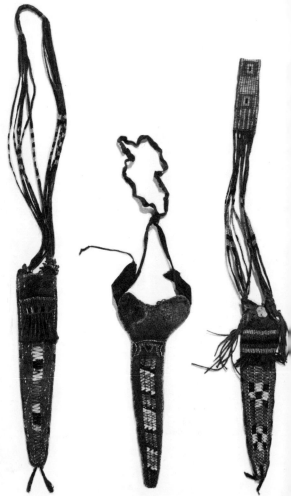

8. Hunting equipment and hunting charms. *Left* (a) Athapaskan net collected at Hay River, Northwest Territories by David T. Hanbury in 1901-2 (length 42 cm); *top (left to right)* (b) Micmac beaver harpoon of caribou antler collected by T. G. B. Lloyd, St George's Bay, Newfoundland (length 15 cm); (c) Beothuk toggle harpoon with slits for the stone point and foreshaft, and two holes for the line, from Lake Bathurst, Newfoundland (length 9.5 cm); (d) fishing line of two-ply vegetable cord and bone gorge (length of gorge 12 cm); (e) Cree beaded charm of a black bear's chin collected by E. Renouf while employed at Great Whale River by the Hudson's Bay Company before 1921 (length 15 cm); *bottom* (f) Cree beaded charm of a Great Northern Diver's head collected by E. Renouf in the 'interior of Rupert river' before 1921 (length 33 cm).

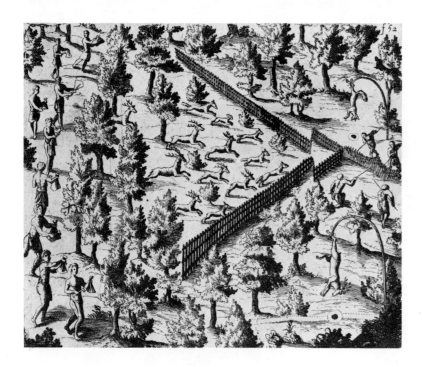

9. Seventeenth-century French engraving illustrating a Huron deer hunt; deer are driven by men with bone clappers into an enclosure where they are trapped and killed with spears; plate v of Samuel de Champlain *Voyages et descouvertures faites en la Nouvelle France depuis l'année 1615 à la fin de l'année 1618*, Paris, 1619.

10. Three skin shot pouches. *Left* Pouch decorated with two horizontal bands of zig-zag line technique quillwork and quilled fringes (length 21 cm); *centre* pouch decorated with two bands of loom-woven quillwork and quill-wrapped fringes (length 21 cm); *right* pouch decorated with two bands of loom-woven quillwork and quill-wrapped loops (length 26 cm).

11. Mid-nineteenth-century engraving of women gathering and threshing wild rice; plate 4 of Henry R. Schoolcraft *Information respecting the History, Condition and Prospects of the Indian Tribes of the United States,* part III, Philadelphia, 1853.

12. Jemima Gibson, Cayuga Iroquois, pounding corn, Six Nations Reserve, Ontario, 13 August 1939.

2 Houses and settlement

Their lodges are fashioned like bowers or arbours, covered with tree-bark, twenty-five to thirty fathoms long more or less, and six wide, leaving in the middle a passage from ten to twelve feet wide . . .
(Champlain p. 122-3)

In the seventeenth century Iroquois villages were semi-permanent settlements often surrounded by stockades as protection at first against neighbouring tribes but later also against European powers. Each might have up to a thousand or more inhabitants living in houses of elm bark constructed over a framework of poles (15). The bark would be flattened, dried, formed into boards and sewn together with vegetable fibre cord. A house ·for a single nuclear family might be 6 metres long, while a longhouse with up to twenty families from a single descent group might be 45 metres long. In a longhouse each family would have its own section, 3 or 4 metres in length, partitioned off from its neighbours. Along the edge of the longhouse were raised bark benches spread with skins for sitting and sleeping.

Tribes entirely dependant on hunting relied on less permanent, often single-family dwellings; these were usually simple round, oval or rectangular structures of poles; they were either rounded or pointed at the top and were known as wigwams (14). Wigwams were covered in mats made of cattail, or rushes, bark, usually birchbark, or sheets of elm or ash bark. The Iroquois used a version of this bark-covered structure, with a triangular base, for shelter during hunting expeditions. Amongst northern tribes tents of moose or caribou skin were used instead of wigwams.

13. Domed Ojibwa wigwams at Sault Ste Marie in 1845–8. They are covered in birchbark and cattail mats. Painting by Paul Kane.

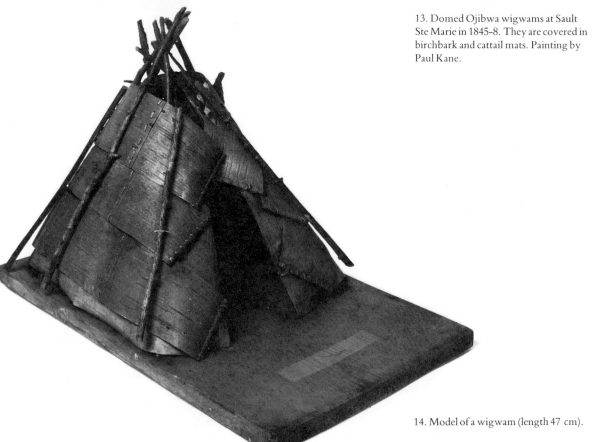

14. Model of a wigwam (length 47 cm).   23

15. Iroquois elm bark covered house in the middle of the nineteenth century; from Lewis H. Morgan *League of the Ho-de'-no-sau-nee, or Iroquois,* Rochester, 1851.

16. The Seneca School on the Buffalo Creek Reservation painted by Dennis Cusick, the son of a Tuscarora chief, in 1821. The scene appears to show two groups of children, perhaps about to be instructed by the men holding weapons. On the right a boy is about to shoot a bird in the tree.

3 Domestic crafts

They make their dishes in which they serve up their meat, and their bowls and pans, out of the knotty excrescences of the maple tree, or any other wood. They fashion their spoons with a tolerable degree of neatness . . .
(Carver p. 234)

Wood carving, which included the manufacture of bowls and spoons, weapons, and some ceremonial paraphernalia, such as lacrosse sticks (25, 26), was the responsibility of the men. They were also in charge of preparing all the dwellings, longhouses, canoes and toboggans, and clearing the land for agriculture. The woman's tasks included all the weaving and embroidery, preparing skin and the production of items made from birchbark; most of the objects illustrated in this book were made by women.

The bark of the white or paper birch was the most important of all available raw materials. It had a wide range of uses, because it was tough, durable and weatherproof. If a large piece of bark was needed, for instance for a canoe, then the tree was cut down and the bark removed. Smaller pieces, for torches, dishes, scrolls or embroidery, would be carefully removed from living trees in spring and early summer. In some areas elm bark was used as an alternative to birch bark.

The other important raw material was skin. Its preparation involved scraping to remove flesh, hair and skin, soaking in a solution of, for instance, mammal brains to help make it pliable, and repeatedly scraping and working to make it soft. Afterwards it might be smoked over a fire to improve its water-resistant qualities and to keep it soft.

Cord was made of a wide variety of fibres including basswood (or the American lime) bark, nettle fibre, and Indian hemp. Utensils made from birchbark were generally sewn with split root rather than cord, and skin was sewn with sinew, which swells when wet and makes the clothing more waterproof. Awls were generally made of bone and needles of large thorns.

Other household containers, such as twined bags, were also made from basswood bark fibre, as well as nettle fibre, Indian hemp, bison wool and yarn obtained from traders or ravelled from blankets. The Ojibwa made checker-weave cedar bark bags to hold wild rice. Woven splint baskets (17) were introduced into North America by Europeans and supplanted the traditional type of basket made from twined vegetable fibre. Mats were made from cattail and cedar bark for use in houses, and cattail mats were also used extensively to cover the frames of wigwams and as wall linings.

17. Dan Denny, Iroquois, making a rim for a splint basket, with his wife holding a partially completed basket in the background. Oneida, Wisconsin, 18 October 1929.

18. An Ojibwa woman weaving a wool sash. She is sitting on a cattail mat. Lac Courte Oreilles Reservation, Wisconsin, 1941.

19. Three items woven from vegetable fibre. *Top* A twined burden strap, or tumpline, brought to England by one of the Iroquois sachems or chiefs who visited London in 1710 (length of headband 50 cm); *centre* a bag from the Great Lakes made from twined vegetable fibre and wool; *bottom* braided vegetable fibre cord of the type which may have been used for tying up prisoners. It is decorated with porcupine quillwork and metal hair-filled cones (length 600 cm).

20. *Top* A cattail mat collected in 1858
(length 92 cm); *bottom (left)* an Ojibwa
twined bag made from the inner bark of the
basswood tree by the 'Indians of Serpent
River, Lake Huron' before 1868 (length
62 cm); *(right)* an Ojibwa checkerweave bag
woven from the inner bark of the white
cedar before 1868 (length 45 cm).

21. Beothuk birchbark dish. This was formerly inscribed: 'Red Indian Meat Dish for Deer's flesh, found in the Chief's tomb at Rd. I. Lake, 1827 by W. E. C.'; it was collected by W. E. Cormack at Red Indian Lake, Newfoundland (length 46 cm).

22. An eighteenth-century flat Ojibwa (?) birchbark pouch decorated with geometric designs in coloured porcupine quillwork. This form of quillwork was used from the middle of the nineteenth century onwards to create figurative designs used on souvenirs such as the model house illustrated in 100 (20×16 cm).

23. Nest of thirty Cree birchbark baskets decorated with quillwork at the rims and sewn with split root. Perhaps collected by Christopher Middleton between 1721 and 1746 (height 35 cm).

24. *Top to bottom* Three wood spoons: (a) Cree spoon collected at Fort Albany, James Bay before 1868 (length 19 cm); (b) Cree spoon collected by E. Renouf while employed by the Hudson's Bay Company at Great Whale River, Quebec, before 1921 (length 14 cm); (c) Ojibwa spoon with its handle carved in the form of a bird and coloured with burnt decoration. It is inscribed 'made by an Indian Chief of the French River Lake Huron August 1856' (length 23 cm); three crooked knives for carving wood: (d) length 28 cm; (e) knife collected before 1862 and inscribed 'Moctagon Knife of Algonquin' (length 22 cm); (f) knife, with a handle carved with animal heads, which was collected by P. W. Dease and Thomas Simpson in 1837-9 (length 28 cm).

25. Two Ojibwa lacrosse sticks. Lacrosse was more than simply a sport, since it had religious overtones, as a game might be sponsored by a man in honour of his guardian spirit (lengths 91 cm *(left)*, 84 cm *(right)*).

26. The St Regis Mohawk lacrosse team in 1867 (?).

Cradles

They have no Notion of cradles for children as the English has, but use other methods, which seem's much better, they make a board wherein they tie the child . . .
(Isham p. 105)

Indian women carried their babies around with them, either attached to cradleboards or else in moss-filled bags; these were originally made of skin but later of trade cloth. Cradleboards consist of a rectangular piece of wood; a hoop over the top protected the head and a bentwood attachment provided support for the feet (28). Attached to its cradleboard, the baby could be easily carried on the mother's back and amongst the Iroquois, for instance, might be suspended from a tree to swing in the breeze while the mother worked in the garden. The boards were often beautifully carved and painted, and the baby might be wrapped in skin or cloth highly decorated with bead and quill attachments (30).

27. Women at Moose Factory, Ontario, with their children. The woman in front is an Inuit (Eskimo) called Husky Annie who was married to a Cree and is using an Indian cradleboard. The Indian women in the background have their babies in moss-filled bags. Photograph taken by Samuel Waller, Anglican schoolmaster at Moose Factory, 1923–1930.

28. Four model cradelboards *Top (left)*
Nineteenth-century Cree or Ojibwa
board (length 47 cm); *(right)* eighteenth-
century Cree board of white cedar,
acquired in about 1740 by John Potts
while working for the Hudson's Bay
Company and associated with James
Isham (length 38 cm); *bottom (left)*
nineteenth-century Cree or Ojibwa
board collected before 1868 (length
23 cm); *(right)* nineteenth-century
Mohawk board collected by George
Brooke of Whimple, Devon
(length 17 cm).

29. Cree velvet baby-bag decorated with beadwork, collected by James A. Heard between 1881 and 1896 (length 48 cm). Traditionally sphagnum moss was used as a type of disposable nappy in such bags.

30. A mid-nineteenth-century Iroquois cradleboard showing the very elaborate beaded cloth wrappings which constituted the outer layer of the babies' coverings; from Lewis H. Morgan *League of the Ho-de'-no-sau-nee, or Iroquois,* Rochester, N.Y., 1851.

31. A late nineteenth-century
photograph of a Minnesota Ojibwa
woman sitting on a canoe with her
children. Behind is a wigwam covered in
birchbark and cattail mats.

4 Clothing

They dress and prepare their skins very well, making their breeches of a moderately large deer-skin, and of another their leggings which reach as high as the waist, with many folds.
(Champlain pp. 131-2)

At the time of European contact clothing often consisted of virtually un-tailored skins, worn with or without fur, depending on the season. The availability of new iron tools such as scissors and needles permitted skin clothing to be cut, fitted and sewn more easily. In the east and around the Great Lakes deer skin was most commonly used, whereas to the north caribou and mooseskin were the primary materials. There were four basic elements of male clothing; leggings (35), breech-clout, moccasins and an outer covering. In the historic period this outer garment was a robe (32), although the Cree and Naskapi wore coats. Woman's clothing was similar, but amongst the Cree a form of dress called the side-fold dress was worn; this was cut from a single skin, folded at the side, and hung from the shoulders by straps. After the arrival of European traders woollen cloth became widely available; in many areas it had virtually replaced skin by the middle of the nineteenth century.

Aboriginal skin clothing was often highly decorated, using a number of different techniques. The most common was painting (40), the paint either applied as a powder, or as a liquid impressed with a bone stamp. Appliqué decoration included porcupine and bird quillwork, and beadwork (35). Moosehair was the most common hair used for embroidery, originally in geometric designs but also, after European contact, often in floral ones. Porcupine quillwork was usually either woven separately on a bow-loom and applied as a strip, or else it was attached to a network of sinew thread sewn into the skin. Originally beads were made of shell, teeth, stone, bone and copper, but after European contact vast quantities of glass beads were introduced from Venice and Bohemia to decorate clothing. As cloth replaced skin an appliqué patchwork of silk ribbon came to be used instead of paint (33).

32. Smoked skin robe. The fringed edge is painted red, and the centre is decorated with a stamped geometric design in black and colourless pigments (140×130 cm).

33. A nineteenth-century painting of a Cree family by Peter Rindisbacher. The man is wearing clothes of woollen cloth decorated with ribbon-work at the edges. Before cloth became available the coat and leggings would have been of skin with painted geometric designs.

34. A pair of mid-nineteenth-century Ojibwa leggings in red and blue cloth decorated with white beadwork and thimbles. An old label describes them as the 'Leggings of the Chief of the Spanish River Indians Lake Huron – Shaubaussin a great conjuror or Wahbunoo Man' (height 61 cm).

35. Cree blue cloth leggings decorated with floral beadwork. Collected by General Sir John Henry Lefroy (1817-90) while making a magnetic survey of Canada in the 1840s.

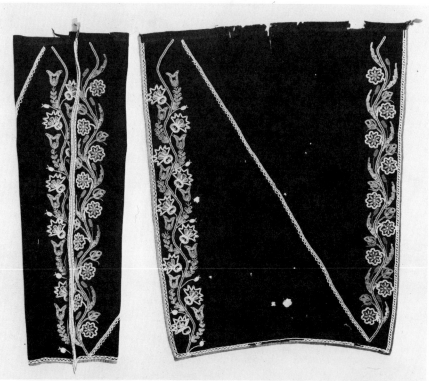

Naskapi coats

The Naskapi of Quebec and Labrador lived by hunting caribou, and used their skins for making tents and clothing. During the winter men wore painted outer coats of caribou skin with the hair left on the inside (37). In the summer they wore painted coats with the hair removed (39, 40). The breech-clout, leggings and moccasins worn with these coats were also made of caribou skin. Originally the coats took the form of a parka with no front opening; later the European style of coat was copied from traders, who would also have supplied the iron tools which permitted the precise cutting and tailoring of the arms and shoulders.

The supreme significance of the caribou hunt may have been reflected in the designs painted on the coats, possibly representing caribou antlers and trees (39). The spirits associated with the caribou were thought to take note of the painted designs and to assist the hunter in his all-important quest for food. The painted designs were applied using a paint stick of bone. The pigments, which included indigo and vermillion obtained from traders and haematite found locally, were mixed with a strained liquid derived from the roe of a sucker fish. This liquid, when used without pigment, produced a rich yellow colour.

36. A Naskapi wearing a cloth cap, with beadwork decoration using the same designs as on the painted summer hunting coats (see 39, 40).

37. A Montagnais-Naskapi hunter wearing a winter parka-type coat, with the fur turned inside, at Lake St John.

39. A Naskapi summer hunting coat made of caribou skin and decorated with painted designs; the cuffs are of red, and the lining of yellow cloth. Collected by General Sir John Henry Lefroy (height 90 cm).

38. This eighteenth-century engraving shows George Cartwright wearing a Naskapi coat painted with linear designs; frontispiece to Cartwright *A journal of transactions and events, during a residence of nearly sixteen years on the coast of Labrador,* vol. I, Newark, 1792.

40. A Naskapi summer hunting coat of caribou skin, decorated with linear painted designs and with quill-wrapped fringes at the shoulders and arms (height 95 cm).

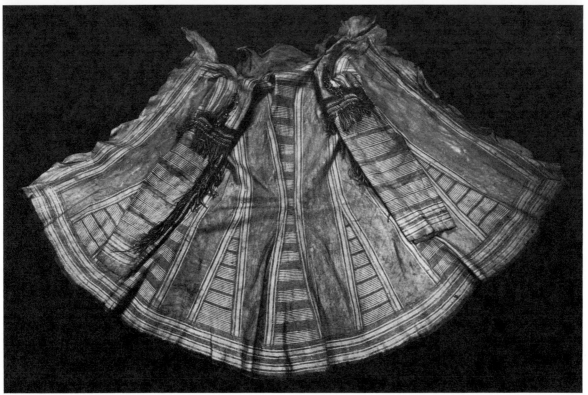

Méti coats

the men Does not Differ much from the women in Dress, they having a Close coate nex't their skin, and a Loose Coate over flying op'n before, with an arsian or clout to cover their private parts . . .
(Isham pp. 110-1)

The Cree, and probably also the Ojibwa, made skin coats modelled on European prototypes. During the nineteenth century Méti artisans, who drew their inspiration as well as their ancestry from European and Indian groups, made coats with extravagant decoration. Some of this was in the form of stamped designs of Algonquian origin, and some of it consisted of floral designs of European origin (43). Méti coats were often heavily decorated with netted and loom-woven quillwork in geometric patterns of Algonquian origin; on other coats the quillwork was of abstract floral design, perhaps inspired by Dakota forms.

41. A nineteenth-century painting by Peter Rindisbacher, including a man on the right, smoking a pipe and wearing a Méti coat decorated with quillwork epaulettes.

42. Méti moose skin coat painted with designs which may represent four men hunting three animals. It is decorated with porcupine quill rosettes, and quillwork strips on the arms and back (height 130 cm).

43. Méti moose skin coat decorated with floral designs (height 130 cm).

Moccasins

The moccason is made of one piece of deer-skin. It is seamed up at the heel, and also in front, above the foot, leaving the bottom of the moccasin without a seam. In front the deer-skin is gathered, in place of being crimped; over this part porcupine quills or beads are worked, in various patterns.
(Morgan p. 360)

Most Northeast moccasins were of two types. They were either gathered along a single seam up the front (44), as in this description of Iroquois moccasins, or else were fitted with a vamp over the instep (47), as in Cree moccasins. Moccasins were perhaps the most important part of Indian clothing, and continued in use long after other articles had been replaced by European equivalents. It is reported at the end of the nineteenth century that the Naskapi were able to make seven pairs from a single caribou skin. As each pair might only last for two to three weeks, an adult would require at least twenty-five pairs a year. In the middle of this century the Mistassini (Cree) made moccasins of caribou and moose skin, and they reckoned to use ten pairs a year.

As with other items of clothing, moccasins were often highly decorated. The tongue, and other parts of the moccasin, might be painted or decorated with appliqué porcupine quillwork (49) or beadwork (48), and occasionally with moose hair embroidery; ankle flaps could be decorated with tassels ending in hair-filled metal cones (46). The numerous forms and styles of decoration of early moccasins are poorly understood.

44. A pair of smoked skin moccasins decorated with quillwork in zig-zag line technique, and partially edged with white beads and hair-filled metal cones (length 23 cm).

45. Sa Ga Yeath Qua Pieth Tow, one of the Mohawk sachems or chiefs who visited London in 1710. He is wearing partially quilled moccasins and is tattooed with elaborate geometric designs. The bear standing behind him indicates his clan.

46. A pair of Ojibwa (?) skin moccasins decorated with porcupine quillwork in zig-zag line technique; the quill-wrapped fringes are terminated in hair-filled metal cones (length 25 cm).

47. A pair of skin moccasins decorated with quillwork in checkerweave and zig-zag line technique. They are said to have been collected in Hudson Bay by a Captain Richards, perhaps either Captain John or Captain Joseph Richards, both of whom worked for the Hudson's Bay Company in the second half of the eighteenth century (length 22 cm).

48. A pair of smoked skin moccasins decorated with quillwork, white beads, gold braid and metal cones (length 27 cm).

49. A single black dyed Huron skin moccasin decorated with panels of loom-woven quillwork which are edged with quillwork in zig-zag line technique, silk ribbon and hair-filled metal cones (length 26.5 cm).

50. Three Huron chiefs wearing highly
decorated moccasins similar to 49. A
lithograph after a painting by Edward
Chatfield, 1825.

5 Personal decoration

They have severall mark's upon their bodies, face and hands, Which they do by pricking the skin with a Needle in the shap'e and for'm they Design, tell the Blood comes, they then take some gun powder, or Coal beat fine, Wich they lay on Rubbing itt for a while tell the bleeding is over, w'ich stands good and never washes out.
(Isham p. 102)

Tattooing, and body-painting, were two of the many ways in which the Woodlands Indians decorated themselves (51). The Iroquois combined elaborate tattoos of linear and geometric forms with realistic representations of clan symbols, such as the turtle or the wolf. Iroquois warriors are said to have worn three painted stripes on each cheek, representing the Six Nations who made up the Iroquois confederacy. Apart from painting and tattooing, the head was also decorated by partial shaving, leaving ridges of hair to which additional feather and hair ornaments could be added (55).

Headgear included hoods and caps known mostly from the cloth examples made and worn by peoples such as the Micmac and Cree. These could be highly decorated, along with other items of clothing, by the common techniques of appliqué quillwork, beadwork, embroidery using moosehair and quill, and fringing. The sashes, belts and garters worn to secure clothing might be made of skin and decorated with any of these techniques. Belts and sashes were also woven from yarn using simple finger-weaving techniques derived from plaiting and braiding; glass beads were often incorporated during the weaving (52). Between 1750 and 1850 beadwork became of paramount importance for decoration, and gradually supplanted quillwork.

A wide variety of ornaments were worn, the most common of which were made of shell and antler. These included gorgets (56), made of circular sections of large univalve shells, strings of wampum (see 72-4), and bent antler armbands (54). After the arrival of the Europeans these materials were replaced by glass and metal. The most common of these were, perhaps, of silver, and included gorgets, armbands, a wide variety of brooches derived from European prototypes, and various types of head-band.

51. An engraving of Hendrick, or King Hendrick, a Mohawk Chief who died fighting for the British against the French in 1775 at the Battle of Lake George. The left side of his face is tattooed with a sun (?).

THUNDERBIRD
and Lightning

Indian life in northeastern North America 1600-1900

MUSEUM OF MANKIND
The Ethnography Department of the British Museum

49

52. Various types of woven ornaments. *Left to right* (a) A head (?) ornament of deer hair. The hair has been sewn in a single strip and wound round a cord in a spiral and resist-dyed red, leaving a small band white. The bottom of the cord is decorated with a quill-wrapped wood cylinder (length 96 cm); (b) netted sash made of thongs wrapped with quillwork in alternating pairs. The design consists of a series of lozenge-shaped panels containing birds in red on a blue background (length 103 cm); (c) quilled belt or sash in zig-zag line technique on smoked skin (length 86 cm); (d) a finger-woven yarn sash, decorated with white beads and resist-dyed red leaving uncoloured bands (length 94 cm); (e) a finger-woven yarn sash decorated with beads at the edges (length 80 cm); (f) sash of yarn strands bound together in open netted technique with quills (length 100 cm); (g) one of a pair of finger-woven yarn garters decorated with beads collected by Lord Amherst in the middle of the eighteenth century (length 22 cm); (h) Iroquois finger-woven yarn sash in five interlocking sections (length 150 cm).

53. *Top to bottom* (a) A pair of netted garters made from thongs wrapped with quillwork in alternating pairs (length 33 cm); (b) pair of garters of quill-wrapped birchbark sewn with sinew and decorated with beads (length 29 cm); (c) pair of finger-woven yarn garters incorporating a white beaded design (length 32 cm); *bottom* (d) a Cree smoked skin belt decorated with two panels of quill-wrapped birchbark strips; collected from around Hudson Bay in the first half of the eighteenth century (length 72 cm); *top right* (e) a pair of beaded finger-woven yarn garter drops resist-dyed red, leaving two uncoloured bands (length 40 cm).

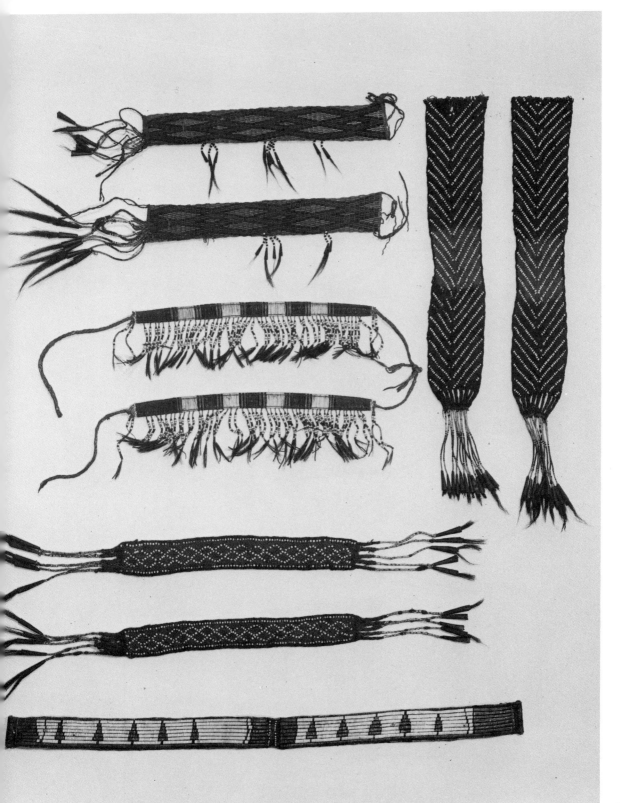

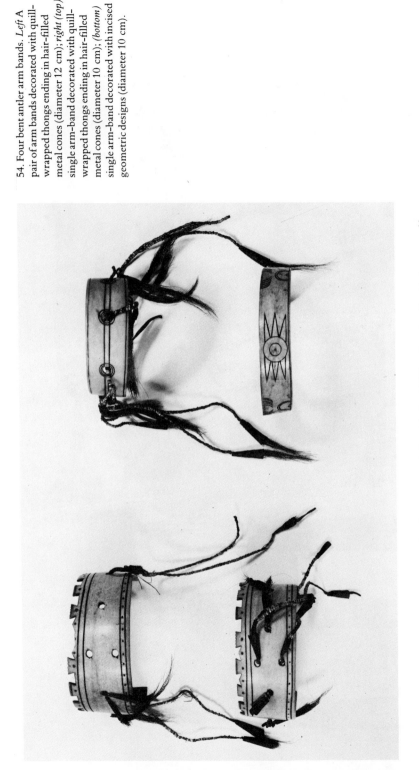

54. Four bent antler arm bands. *Left* A pair of arm bands decorated with quill-wrapped thongs ending in hair-filled metal cones (diameter 12 cm); *right (top)* single arm-band decorated with quill-wrapped thongs ending in hair-filled metal cones (diameter 10 cm); *(bottom)* single arm-band decorated with incised geometric designs (diameter 10 cm).

55. Head and neck ornaments. *Left to right (top)* (a) Two lengths of braided grass used by Ojibwa women from around Lake Huron to decorate their hair. Collected before 1868 (length of shank 27 cm); (b) Beothuk bone ornament with incised design (length 12 cm); (c) two Naskapi ear ornaments used by young girls. Collected before 1921 by E. Renouf while employed by the Hudson's Bay Company at Great Whale River (dimensions of beaded panels 15×9 cm); *(bottom)* (d) two silver gorgets engraved with a deer and a bird, acquired in Montreal before 1862 (diameters 10.5, 8 cm); (e) ornament perhaps for attaching to a ridge of hair on an otherwise shaven head consisting of a panel of loom-woven quillwork backed with skin with a fringe of beads at one end and a braided tie at the other (length 9 cm); (f) a head ornament for a chief, collected before 1862, consisting of three quill-wrapped wood splints incorporating hair and feathers at the end, and a single feather (maximum length 40 cm).

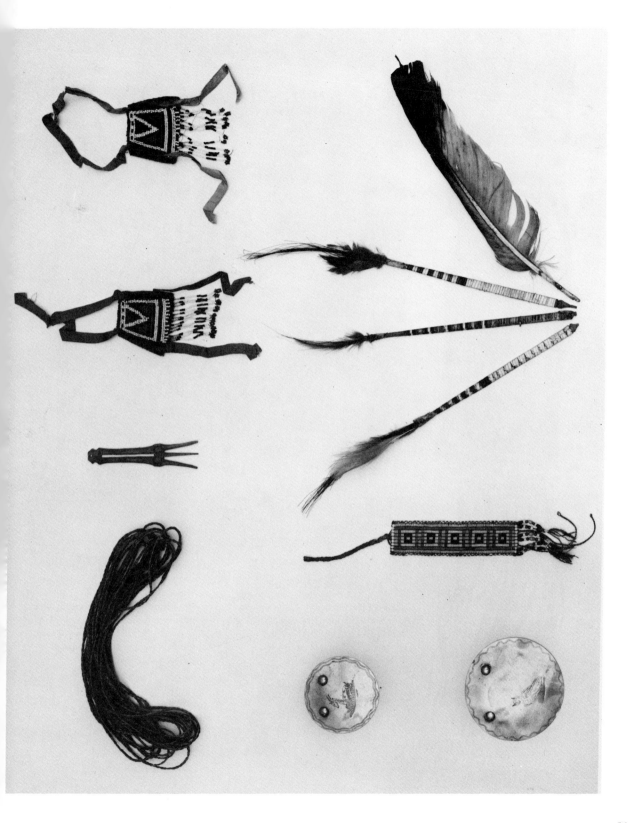

56. An Ottawa ornament consisting of a shell gorget attached with two shoulder straps of imitation glass wampum to two panels of netted quill thongs each representing Thunderbirds with lightning (length 120 cm).

57. An Ottawa man wearing a large metal gorget representing the sun; he has painted or tattooed decoration on his left cheek and forehead, and strings of beads through his ears and nose; from the 'Codex Canadensis', c.1700.

6 Religion

'Hail, hail, hail. Thou who hast created all things, who rulest all things, and who givest laws and commands to they creatures, listen to our words. We now obey thy commands. That which thou hast made is returning unto thee. It is rising to thee, by which it will apear that our words are true.'
Prayer to the Great Spirit at the time of the sacrifice of a dog (with some leaves of tobacco) at the Midwinter Ceremony of the Iroquois. (Morgan, p. 218)

The Northeastern peoples believed in a multitude of spirits who inhabited the plants and animals, rocks and rivers, wind, rain and stars, and all other natural phenomena. In overall control of these spirits was a loosely defined paramount spirit. It was necessary for every individual to remain in harmony with these spirits, and especially those which gave form and substance to the food sources on which man depended. Religious observance consisted of minor ceremonies, which were frequently repeated and often involved the sacrifice of small amounts of tobacco or food, designed to propriate spirits.

Amongst the Ojibwa the spirit world was loosely divided into an Upper World inhabited by benign spirits representing, for instance, the Sun and Moon, and Thunderbirds, and the Under World. Evil spirits included Underwater Panthers, and a cannibal giant, called the Windigo, who searched for people to eat in the winter. Each individual possessed a guardian spirit, originally sought out in a vision quest or dream at an early age, who protected and aided him throughout this life. Other beliefs enabled individuals, sometimes known colloquially as Medicine Men, to call on the spirit world for help in curing the sick and in performing other duties. Amongst the Ojibwa and other Great Lakes Algonquians a curing society, called the Mide or Midewiwin Society, was organised by recognised priests and their assistants.

The Iroquoian peoples also believed in a world full of spirits who exerted a day-to-day control over men. For the Huron the most important of these spirits (*oki*) was the spirit of the sky, who controlled the seasons and natural phenomena. Some Huron spirits had a partially realistic form; amongst these were a woman, *ataensic,* associated with the Moon, and her grandson, *iouskeha,* identified with the Sun. Thunderbirds or Thunderers (*onditachiaé*) were conceived as half-human, half-turkey cocks; they represented the spirit of rain, and of thunder and lightning. The Iroquois proper possessed a similar spirit world, propitiated in a series of ceremonies related to the annual food cycle, and medicine societies, such as the False-Face Society, which helped diagnose and prevent disease.

Iroquois religion

Traditional Iroquois religion, the Longhouse Religion, today follows the early-nineteenth-century Code of Handsome Lake, a Seneca sachem and prophet. Handsome Lake combined the ancient elements of Iroquois religion in a new framework suited to the period of decay and disintegration which followed the American destruction of Iroquois power in the late eighteenth century.

Iroquois religion centres on rituals thanking the Great Spirit, *hä-wen-ne'-yu,* for the existence of creatures and beings, both real and mythological, on which life depends. As befits a people with a mixed economy, some of these spirits were to do with hunting, others with agriculture. Today the annual agricultural cycle provides most of the basis for religion in a series of seasonal festivals which express gratitude and thanks to the Great Spirit. Among these festivals are: the Maple Festival, giving thanks to the maple for yielding up its sweetness; the Planting Festival, designed to request the Great Spirit to bless seed; the Wild Strawberry Festival intended as a thanksgiving for the first wild fruits; the Green Corn Festival celebrating the ripening of maize, beans and squash; the Harvest Festival; and the Midwinter or New Year Festival (58).

These festivals are sometimes combined with curing rituals. Curing is carried out by people who have had a vision or dream of False Faces, grotesque creatures with the power to cause and cure illness, particularly to do with the head, shoulders and joints.

People with this experience became members of the False-Face Society which carries out cures of individuals and performs communal rituals for the general prevention of disease. A second curing society, the Husk-Face Society associated with spirits to do with farming rather than the forest, holds curing dances during the Midwinter Festival.

58. Sherman Red Eye driving a Packard before a False-Face ceremony of the Allegany Seneca, 1 August 1934.

59. A house-to-house visitation of
people wearing False-Face masks during
the Midwinter Festival, 1908.

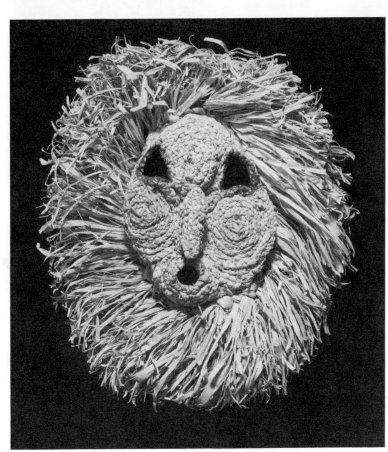

60. An Iroquois Corn-Husk mask made
from coiled braids of maize husks sewn
together with cotton (height 35 cm).

LEFT
61. False-Face mask carved on a living basswood tree in 1909 on the Cattaraugus Seneca reservation, New York.

RIGHT
62. A Seneca False-Face mask, from the Cattaraugus reservation; the hair is horse-hair still attached to skin, and the eyes are surrounded by metal plates (height 27 cm).

63. Iroquois ceremonial equipment. *Top (left to right)* (a) An eighteenth-century hickory stick in the form of a snake used to cause vomiting (length 82 cm); (b) another vomiting stick brought to England in 1710 by the four sachems (length 36 cm); (c) paddle used for stirring corn mush inscribed 'J K S MAKER' (length 61 cm); (d) hickory stick (?) used perhaps in the moccasin game played at the time of mourning (length 67 cm); (e) Seneca turtle-shell rattle (length 50 cm); *bottom* (f) leg rattle of split deer hooves attached with thongs to a skin strip (length 65 cm).

The Midewiwin

The Midewiwin, or Medicine Dance, of the central Algonquian peoples arose as a religious response to the disruption and changes wrought by the European fur trade in the seventeenth century. It may be regarded as a set of rituals forming a cult in which traditional shamanism was fused with an organisation intent on preserving traditional lore in a period of extreme uncertainty and change.

The Midewiwin is performed by a society, the Mide Society, with a limited number of members who possess an organised series of rituals which are believed to have the power, through the use of herbs, missiles and medicine bundles, to kill and to cure people. Membership of the Society is achieved following a long period of instruction by a high-ranking member knowledgeable in tribal myths, traditions and folklore. Much of this knowledge is inscribed onto birchbark scrolls, as are the songs and dances performed at meetings of the Society.

The Midewiwin still exists in Ojibwa and other Great Lakes communities. In some places the Society is regarded as a benevolent source of tribal traditions, and in others its members are thought of as sorcerers. Participation in the Society reaffirms group solidarity and provides explanations for the misfortunes of individuals and communities.

64. An imaginative mid-nineteenth-century engraving showing a communal curing ceremony in progress; plate 31 of Henry R Schoolcraft *Archives of Aboriginal Knowledge,* vol. VI, Philadelphia, 1860.

65. European military drum collected in the 1850s by Henry Christy in Hudson's Bay Territory. This was probably used by an Ojibwa, and the upper half is painted with figures including four Thunderbirds (diameter 46 cm).

66. Wooden drum engraved with two Underwater Panthers and painted red and black. This was collected in the 1850s near Fort Carlton, Saskatchewan, with the songboard in 67 (height 43 cm).

LEFT
67. Wooden songboard engraved with mnemonic devices consisting of pairs of male and female animals; those in the centre are moose (height 48 cm).

RIGHT
68. Ojibwa pouch made of a whole beaver skin and lined with printed cotton cloth; the tail is covered with wool cloth and decorated with white beads. Collected from the 'Spanish River Indians', Lake Huron, before 1868 (length 120 cm).

69. Birchbark Mide scroll collected in Minnesota by an Episcopalian (Anglican) Missionary from an Ojibwa, Bad Boy, between 1852 and 1858 (length 65 cm).

64

70. Kahkewanquonaby – a Canadian Chief. This photograph of the Reverend Peter Jones, a half-Mississauga (Ojibwa) and half-Welsh Weslyan Missionary, was taken in Scotland in 1844–5 and shows a mixture of traditional and semi-traditional costume including a black-dyed skin pouch embroidered with a Thunderbird.

71. Six decorated pouches. *Top (left to right)* (a) Black dyed skin shot (?) pouch decorated with horizontal panels of loom-woven quillwork (16×16 cm); (b) twined eighteenth-century Huron bag of Indian hemp with false embroidered decoration in moosehair (dimensions 12×12.5 cm); (c) black dyed Huron pouch decorated in abstract floral designs in moosehair (height 23 cm); (d) black dyed Ojibwa or Ottawa bag decorated with quillwork and embroidered with a Thunderbird holding an animal in its left claw (height 45 cm); *bottom (left)* (e) black dyed Ojibwa or Ottawa bag decorated with quillwork and embroidered with two Thunderbirds with lightning emerging from two of their claws (31×26 cm); *(right)* (f) smoked skin Ojibwa or Ottawa bag decorated with quillwork and embroidered with a Thunderbird (height 43 cm).

7 Ceremony and ritual

Wampum

If this Wampum Peak *be black or purple, as some Part of that Shell is, then it is twice the value. This the* Indians *grind on Stones and other things till they make it current . . .*
(John Lawson, 1714, quoted in Orchard, 1929 p. 63)

Before European contact shell beads were flat and disc-shaped so that they could be drilled easily from both sides. The acquisition of European tools permitted the manufacture of large quantities of cylindrical shell beads drilled through the centre known as *wampum* (literally 'a white string of shell beads'). These beads, made of white and also purple shell, were used as decoration for clothing and weapons, and worn in the form of sashes, small hats and aprons (72), but they had a wider significance than mere decoration, since they were used extensively as currency, and in ritual and ceremony. They were usually made from a clam shell (*Venus mercenaria*), which is white with a thin purple edge, although purple was the more valuable form. Imitation wampum of glass was imported from Europe.

In ceremonial use wampum was strung into strands and bunches, which could be used to convey information by specific combinations of purple and white beads. The death of an important chief, for example, among the Iroquois would be announced by sending a string of purple beads to other tribes. Wampum was also made into belts which were used to convey peaceful, warlike or other intentions between tribes. The belts were usually mainly of one colour, with designs symbolic of their function in the other colour. White was auspicious and conveyed ideas of peace and good intent, whereas purple conveyed hostility, sadness and death. A white belt might therefore express an alliance or peace, and a purple one a declaration of war.

72. Objects decorated with wampum: (a) an eighteenth-century bag decorated with a panel of imitation glass wampum (20×18 cm); (b) a birchbark scroll, with an ink inscription, given by the Huron of Lorette to the Marquess of Lorne on the occasion of his visit while Governor General of Canada on 22 August 1883. At each corner a small piece of skin is attached and decorated with a few pieces of wampum (34×34 cm); (c) a skin moccasin decorated with wampum (length 25 cm); (d) an eighteenth-century sash of black and white beads. Although the beads are spherical they are grouped in pairs between thin skin strips in order, perhaps, to create the general appearance of a wampum belt (length 115 cm); (e) a belt of wampum constructed with seventeen thongs used as warps. Attached is a turtle made of skin which is also decorated with shell beads (length 65 cm).

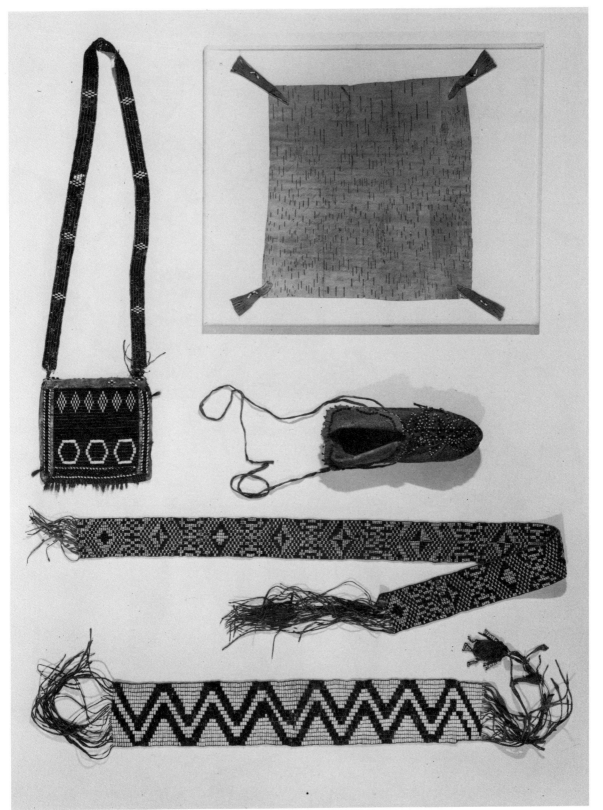

73. A seventeenth-century Delaware
family decorated with a variety of
different ornaments of wampum as
depicted in a stylised manner by Peter
Mårtensson Lindeström in 1653.

74. A painting of a seventeenth-century
Niantic sachem or chief from Rhode
Island called Ninigret. He is wearing
ornaments of wampum and a white
shell gorget.

Smoking pipes and calumets

. . . the ceremony of smoking is practised with much solemnity, previous to the discussion or execution of any transaction of importance.
(Heriot p. 473)

Tobacco was used primarily in a ritual context in North America. Smoking was an activity undertaken not so much for pleasure as a means of propitiating personal and natural spirits (75), and for establishing bonds between individuals and groups of people. A traveller or trader would smoke tobacco with strangers to show peaceful intentions; tobacco would be smoked as an offering to important natural spirits to obtain favourable weather or to bring rain. Pipes would also be smoked by groups of people about to embark on a war, or by tribes making treaties, alliances or establishing peace.

Pipe bowls were made from a wide variety of materials: soapstone, sandstone, slate and catlinite, a red claystone. Wood was occasionally used among the Ojibwa and Iroquois, and before European contact the Huron and Iroquois had made pipes of clay. The Naskapi used river pebbles of fine grained sandstone for their pipe bowls; stones shot through with lines of different colours were the most highly valued. Pipes were often carved with human and animal figures which might represent personal spirits of the owner or clan symbols. They usually faced the user, as the decoration was intended for the user's benefit. In the eighteenth and nineteenth centuries lead came to be used for decorative inlay, particularly on stone pipes.

The pipe bowls were fitted with calumets, long, highly decorated stems or reeds. These were decorated with painted or carved designs; feathers were attached to indicate the special significance of the pipe. The Ojibwa, for example, might use the feathers of the red Pileated woodpecker, associated with Thunderbirds, to signify the fight against underworld spirits.

75. An Indian smoking his pipe in honour of his personal spirit, the sun; from the 'Codex Canadensis', *c.*1700.

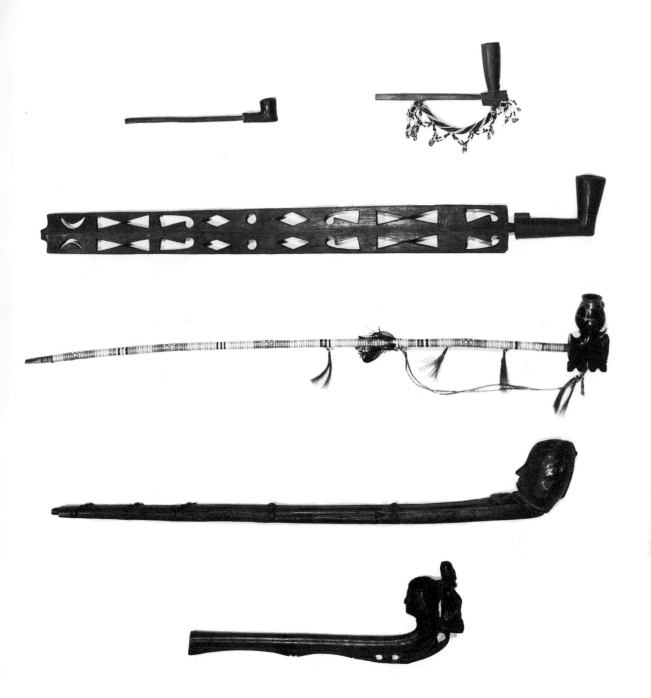

76. *Top right* (a) Naskapi pipe collected by E. Renouf at Great Whale River, Quebec, when a Hudson's Bay Company employee (length 18 cm); *top left* (b) Cree pipe inscribed on the bowl 'To Corporal E. Morell Cree Indian Pipe Battle for North-West Territory Rebellion Canada 1885 May 24 from Chief Poundmaker' (length 21 cm); (c) an Ojibwa calumet brought to England in 1825 by Bryan Mullanphy, (1809-51) of Baltimore and St Louis (length 79 cm); (d) an Ojibwa calumet with a quill-wrapped stem and a lead-inlaid stone bowl (length 79 cm); (e) an Ojibwa calumet of wood – the bowl is carved as a human head facing the smoker (length 51 cm); (f) an Iroquois wood pipe from the first half of the eighteenth-century. The bowl is carved as a human head, with a human figure wearing a copper arm-band sitting behind (length 37 cm).

77. Three stone pipe bowls. *Top (left)*
Pipe bowl carved with a dog or wolf
(length 14 cm) *(right)* Iroquois pipe bowl
carved with figures including a turtle,
collected near Niagara (height 7 cm);
bottom pipe bowl found on the battlefield
of Greenwood Lake, New Jersey
(length 13 cm).

8 Transport

their snow shoes are of Different form's and sizes, some being 7 and 8 foot Long, a small Comfort for a man to Carry upon his feet Severall months up to the Knees in Snow . . .
(Isham pp. 137-8)

Transportation in the northeast was either by foot or by canoe, although plank toboggans drawn by dogs were, and still are, used by some tribes. Two devices aided transportation on foot; one was the snow shoe (83), of bent-wood construction and laced with rawhide, gut or sinew. The other was the burden strap (80), or tumpline, woven from vegetable fibres such as Indian hemp and often decorated with moosehair.

Canoes were constructed from wood frames covered with bark, usually, but not always, birchbark (82). Construction began by laying out a large piece of bark on a building bed which was shaped in the form that the hull was to take. The canoe might be constructed using a building frame; alternatively the gunwales could be put together first and used to shape the canoe. The birchbark for the covering would be cut and sewn with spruce root, and the seams covered in spruce gum. The interior would be fitted with a sheathing of, for instance, white cedar splints and ribs of spruce. Paddles were made of splints of maple, spruce, white cedar and other woods.

78. A model of a Cree (?) toboggan (length 44 cm).

79. An imaginative engraving illustrating the use of burden straps, toboggans and snow shoes. The engraver has omitted the fur clothing which would have been worn in snow, and has made the snow shoes very small. Burden straps were used for carrying loads and, according to Lafitau, were worn across the chest by men and around the forehead by women; detail from plate 11 of Joseph François Lafitau *Moeurs des sauvages ameriquaines*, vol. 2, Paris, 1724.

80. Three burden straps, perhaps of Indian hemp; the central sections are twined and decorated with moosehair in false embroidery, while the ties are braided. *Top* Iroquois burden strap brought to London by the sachems who visited Queen Anne in 1710 (length of central section 50 cm); *centre* burden strap, the central section edged with beads (length of central section 50 cm); *bottom* burden strap, the central section edged with beads (length of central section 60 cm).

75

ABOVE
81. Model Ottawa canoe collected before
1862 (length 90 cm).

BELOW
82. Ojibwa Indians constructing a canoe
in Minnesota in the late nineteenth
century.

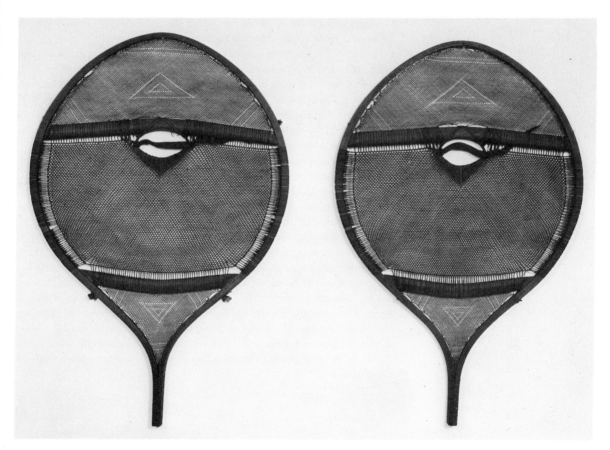

83. A pair of Naspaki swallow tail snow shoes. The frame is made from a single piece of wood with two wooden cross-bars; the hexagonal weave mesh of rawhide incorporates geometric designs (length 82 cm).

9 Warfare

. . . the existence of the war was indicated by a tomahawk painted red, ornamented with red feathers, and with black wampum, struck in the war-post in each village of the League.
(Morgan p. 339)

Among isolated hunting tribes warfare was not an important aspect of life. Where it did exist, particularly among the Iroquoian-speaking peoples, it was very different from European war. The destruction of property, killing and conquest were less important than personal achievement, particularly the acquisition of captives during raids. Men taken in raids would be bound and lead back to the captor's village, where they would be adopted by a family who had suffered a loss in war. The captive might be retained by the family, or be tortured to death by fire and other means. If the captive was to die he would be well fed, dressed in fine robes and wampum, and would be expected to sing and express no discomfort throughout his ordeal. Although extremely cruel, this form of death, and the cannibalism which followed, was highly ritualised and suggested a form of sacrifice in which the power and other attributes of the captive were acquired by his tormentors.

The basis of war altered radically after the arrival of the French, Dutch and British. European weapons and trade goods, and the competition for furs, intensified war, bringing a new emphasis on the wholesale destruction of property and on genocide. In the early seventeenth century the Huron were not permitted to acquire firearms by their French allies. The Iroquois, however, were able to do so, and therefore had the means to destroy the Huron, their enemies, during the 1640s.

In the colonial wars of the seventeenth and eighteenth centuries Indian tribes were important allies of the European protagonists. The Iroquois generally supported the British, and Algonquian-speaking peoples the French. As a result of the American Revolution the Iroquois allies of Britain suffered severely at the hands of the American general, John Sullivan. Many Iroquois fled to Canada at this time.

The most important aboriginal weapons were bows and arrows, the ball-headed club and various forms of stone clubs (90), usually called tomahawks. These were generally replaced by iron and steel hatchets, pipe-tomahawks, and by firearms where available. War exploits were engraved on clubs and depicted in paintings on the inside of dwellings. Scalps removed from the dead, or from tortured victims, were regarded both as trophies and as objects of spiritual power. European warfare spread and secularised the collection of scalps, turning an article of some religious significance into one merely of financial worth.

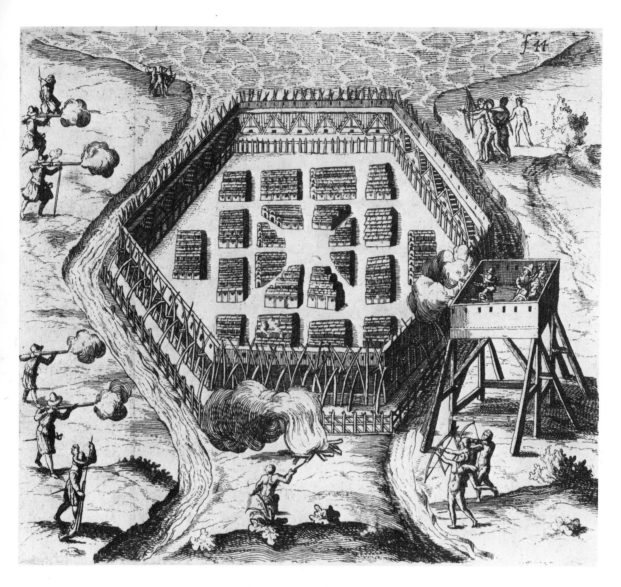

84. A stylised French engraving
illustrating an Iroquois village under
seige by Samuel de Champlain and his
Huron and Algonquin allies in 1615;
plate IV of Champlain *Voyages et
descouvertures faites en la Nouvelle France
depuis l'année 1615 à la fin de l'année 1618*,
Paris, 1619.

85. A watercolour of 1760 by Thomas Davies showing four Royal Artillery boats taking a French ship on the St Lawrence. In the foreground is an Indian village of bark-covered longhouses and a European fort.

86. The centre of the composite engraving below shows two Jesuits, Jean de Brébeuf and Gabriel Lalemant, being killed at the stake by Iroquois at Taenhatentaron in March 1649. The Iroquois had by this time almost completely dispersed the Huron and were, in the torture of these two priests, aided by Huron whom they had adopted and who blamed the Jesuits for the destruction of their country. Scenes at the back and on the left show other French and Indian martyrs from this period; from François du Creux *Historia Canadensis*, Paris, 1664.

80

87. Objects associated with war. *Top (left)* A scalp, painted red and stretched on a wood hoop decorated with quills and split root (diameter 20.5 cm); *(right)* a powder horn with a horn measure, brush, turned wood base, and an Indian yarn strap decorated with beadwork (length of powder horn 35 cm); *bottom (left)* steel pipe-tomahawk, collected before 1830 (length 40 cm); *(right)* an English (?) knife with a black dyed skin sheath decorated with quillwork (length 22 cm);

88. Kitchie-ogi-maw, a Menominee chief painted in 1845 by Paul Kane during a
gathering of Indians waiting to receive the annual payment of treaty money from the
United States government. He is wearing a quilled knife sheath holding a knife of
English manufacture (?) and has a pipe-tomahawk of the type probably made in
Birmingham or Sheffield for the Indian trade of the Hudson's Bay Company.

89. Skin map of the Ohio valley which
may show grants of land by Indians.
Brought to England by
Bryan Mullanphy, 1825.

90. Ball-headed and gunstock clubs. *Top to bottom* Ojibwa club carved with the figure of a mammal (length 54 cm); Huron club carved with an incised design representing a Thunderer striking a man, and inlaid with glass beads (length 54 cm); ball-headed club (length 67 cm); gunstock club (length 70 cm); Ojibwa gunstock club collected before 1821 (length 62 cm).

91. A detail from a painting by Benjamin West, dated 1770, of the death of General Wolfe at Quebec in 1759, showing an Indian with realistic costume and accoutrements.

92. A stylised seventeenth-century French engraving of an Ottawa prepared for war. The shield is said to have been made of tanned leather; plate III, fig. c of Samuel de Champlain *Voyages et descouvertures faites en la Nouvelle France depuis l'annéee 1615 à la fin de l'année 1618*, Paris, 1619.

93. Two finger-woven yarn bags decorated with beadwork (*left* 28×20 cm, *right* 30×30 cm).

94. A drawing by Robert Adam for the monument to Roger Townshend, killed at the battle of Ticonderoga. The monument was erected in Westminster Abbey in 1761. The moccasins, leggings and other costume details in the sketch are all realistic; the fleur-de-lis on the powder horn suggest that the Indian represents the vanquished Indian allies of France.

95. Three peace medals and a token used in the fur trade. Medals were presented by European powers and their successor states to Indian chiefs as marks of allegiance. *Top to bottom* A bronze medal of Louis XIV of 1693 of the type thought to have been given to Indians; a silver medal of George II of 1757 showing a white man smoking a calumet with an Indian; a late eighteenth-century engraved American silver medal showing George Washington and, on the reverse, an Indian sitting under a column with thirteen hands representing the thirteen American states; a token of 1820 of the North West Company, one of the few rivals to the Hudson's Bay Company in British North America in the early nineteenth century. Furs were exchanged for tokens which could then be used to purchase supplies from the company.

10 Objects made for sale

When I found the shops at Niagara Falls full of dainty Indian beadwork, and stunning moccasins, and equally stunning toy figures . . . I was filled with emotion. (Twain p. 19)

Many museum artefacts, particularly those of skin and birchbark, were acquired when new as souvenirs and never used. Many more were deliberately made for sale and had no other Indian use. Most common of these are models of snow shoes and canoes, and a huge range of beaded cloth and quilled birchbark and sweetgrass artefacts (97). These included replicas of European-American household items such as scissor cases, card trays, baskets, pouches and boxes, and also models of houses (100). Vast quantities of these things were sold to nineteenth-century tourists, particularly at Niagara Falls. Indian artists also produced other types of embroidered items for the market; these included beaded costumes for Wild West shows and Masonic use (96), and floral moosehair-embroidered cloth chair covers and table cloths for use in Victorian houses. The Micmac, who made a wide range of souvenir boxes in the nineteenth century, also produced beautiful quilled birchbark panels to be incorporated in tables, chairs and fire screens. Floral embroidery in moosehair was encouraged in French convents in Quebec, where, during the eighteenth century, Indian girls were taught to embroider in the European manner. This survived into the nineteenth century when the Huron were still making large quantities of beautifully embroidered moccasins (99). Other peoples, such as the Micmac, retained their traditional designs in the quillwork artefacts made for sale.

96. Mountain Eagle and his family of Iroquois Indians. A late-nineteenth-century photograph by Jacob A. Riis of Indians making beadwork, probably for sale or use in a travelling Indian exhibition, in a New York slum tenement.

97. Ojibwa selling souvenirs at Parry Sound, Ontario, 1928. The souvenirs include birchbark boxes and canoes decorated with porcupine quillwork, and sweetgrass trays.

98. Knives, knife sheaths and a wall
ornament decorated with floral
embroidery. *Left to right* Huron sheath
decorated with a panel of black dyed skin
worked with moosehair embroidery
(length 30 cm); a Huron knife and
sheath; the sheath is decorated with
moosehair embroidery and beadwork
(length 28 cm); a knife and sheath; the
sheath decorated with floral quillwork
(length 27 cm); Huron wall decoration in
the form of the skin and hoof of a caribou
leg decorated with two panels of black
dyed skin embroidered in moosehair
(length 50 cm); knife with birchbark
sheath covered in skin embroidered in
silk (length 42 cm).

99. A pair of Huron moosehair
embroidered shoes; the uppers are made
from black dyed skin and are stitched to
soles and heels of commercially tanned
leather (?) (length 20 cm).

100. A birchbark model of a house
decorated with geometric and floral
designs, as well as realistic
representations of windows, including
dormer windows. Collected between
1877 and 1879 by Father E. I. Purbrick,
S.J. (length 23 cm).

Sources of the illustrations

Unless otherwise stated the objects and illustrations in this book are from the Museum of Mankind (Department of Ethnography, British Museum). The author and publishers are grateful to the copyright holders for permission to reproduce the photographs.

1. Thomas Gilcrease Institute of American History and Art, Tulsa.
2. Vincent O. Erickson, National Museum of Man; Ottawa.
3. National Gallery of Canada, Ottawa.
4. Photograph by Charles A. Zimmerman, St Paul; Blackmore Collection B/2935.
5. L 1939.6-10.8.
6. (a) 1977 Am 1 1 (presented by Sir John Winnifrith, Governor of the New England Company); (b) +9124 (presented to the Christy collection by T. G. B. Lloyd); (c) +4961 (presented to the Christy collection by the Director of the Royal Botanic Gardens, Kew); (d) 1935.7-10.2 (presented by Miss Dollman in 1935).
7. (a) Christy collection 2587, 2588, St 780; (b) 1932.3-7.1; (c) 1949 Am 22 134; (d) Christy collection 2652.
8. (a) 1903. 6-15.11 (presented by David T. Hanbury); (b) 9125 (presented to the Christy collection by T. G. B. Lloyd); (c) Ll.2 (presented by T. G. B. Lloyd); (d) Sl 1736 (presented to the Sloane collection by John Winthrop (1681-1747); (e, f) 1921.10-4.181, 212 (presented by E. Renouf).
9. British Library Board.
10. 1921.10-14.98, 96 (acquired from the Yorkshire Philosophical Society Museum); Christy collection 2584.
12. William N. Fenton.
13. Royal Ontario Museum, Toronto.
14. +4953 (presented to the Christy collection by the Director of the Royal Botanic Gardens, Kew, in 1888).
16. Rock Foundation, New York.
17. Milwaukee Public Museum.
18. Milwaukee Public Museum.
19. Sloane collection Sl 574; on loan from Stonyhurst College; +6984 (acquired from 'Pickering' and presented to the Christy collection by Sir A. W. Franks).

20. 1960 Am 10 9 (presented by the Director of the Royal Botanic Gardens, Kew); Christy collection 1589, 584.
21. 6975 (presented to the Christy collection by the Royal Institution).
22. 1949 Am 22 142.
23. Sloane collection Sl 2065.
24. (a) 1494; (b) 1921.10-4.200 (presented by E. Renouf); (c) Christy collection St 792; (d) 96.480 (presented to the Christy collection by Sir A. W. Franks); Christy collection (e) St 783; (f) 2574.
25. Christy collection +5169, +5168.
26. Blackmore collection A40/2016.
27. Ipswich Museum.
28. 1944 Am 2 250 (acquired by H. Beasley from the Colonial and Continental Church Society and presented by Mrs H. Beasley); Sloane collection Sl 2040; Christy collection 2573; Q79 Am 9.
29. 1949 Am 6 3 (presented by Major John Pares and Lieutenant-Colonel William Pares).
31. Photograph by Charles A. Zimmerman, St Paul. Blackmore collection B/2937.
32. 1944 Am 2 219 (acquired by H. Beasley from the Royal Artillery Museum, Woolwich, and presented by Mrs H. Beasley).
33. Public Archives of Canada, Ottawa.
34. Christy collection 2575.
35. On loan from Mrs J. H. Loch and Mr J. D. Boles.
36. Photograph by Robert Flaherty; © 1974/1979 The Robert and Frances Flaherty Study Center, School of Theology at Claremont, California, and Royal Ontario Museum, Toronto.
37. Frank G. Speck papers, Peabody Museum, Salem.
39. On loan from Mrs J. H. Loch and Mr J. D. Boles.
40. 2613 (acquired by the Christy collection from the Royal United Services Museum before 1868).
41. West Point Museum, New York.
42. 7400 (presented to the Christy collection by Sir A. W. Franks).
43. 1954 W Am 5 965 (presented by the Trustees of the Wellcome Museum).
44. 1921.10-14.84 (acquired from the Yorkshire Philosophical Society Museum).

46. 1963 Am 5 2.
47. Christy collection 2589.
48. Christy collection St 775.
49. 1972 Am 13 13 (presented by Mrs A. W. Fuller).
50. Public Archives of Canada, Ottawa.
51. British Museum (Department of Prints and Drawings).
52. (a) +6996 (acquired from 'Pickering' and presented to the Christy collection by Sir A. W. Franks); (b) 1944 Am 2 226 (presented by Mrs H. Beasley); (c) 96.16 (presented to the Christy collection by Sir A. W. Franks); Christy collection (d) 2622; (e) 2579; (f) 2643; (g) 1972 Am 13 15 (presented by Mrs A. W. Fuller); (h) 1942 Am 6 1 (presented by Lionel Ridout).
53. (a) Christy collection 2581; (b) 1944 Am 2 244 (presented by Mrs H. Beasley); Christy collection 2578; (d) Sloane collection Sl 2043; Christy collection 2580.
54. Q79 Am 7, 6; Christy collection 9379.
55. (a) Christy collection 2642; (b) Ll3 (presented by T. G. B. Lloyd); (c) 1921.10-4.186 (presented by E. Renouf); Christy collection (d) St 799; (e) 2585; (f) St 774.
56. +6992 (acquired from 'Pickering' and presented to the Christy collection by Sir A. W. Franks).
57. Thomas Gilcrease Institute of American History and Art, Tulsa.
58. Photograph by A. C. Parker (?), Rochester Museum and Science Center.
59. William N. Fenton.
60. 1977 Am 36 1.
61. Rochester Museum and Science Center.
62. 1925.12-7.1.
63. Sloane collection (a) Sl 1532; (b) Sl 572; (c) +4959 (presented to the Christy collection in 1888 by the Director of the Royal Botanic Gardens, Kew); (d) 1959 Am 7 6 (acquired from the Commonwealth and Colonial Church Society); (e)

1900-236 (presented by the Rev. S. C. Freer); (f) +8512 (presented to the Christy collection by Sir A. W. Franks).
65. Christy collection 2144.
66. 2223 (presented to the Christy collection by the Director of the Royal Botanic Gardens, Kew).
67. 2252 (presented to the Christy collection by the Director of the Royal Botanic Gardens, Kew).
68. Christy collection 1133.
69. 1949 Am 22 169.
70. Hill-Adamson album, National Portrait Gallery.
71. (a) 1946 Am 15 1; (b) Sloane collection Sl 203; (c) 1921.10-14.100 (acquired from the Yorkshire Philosophical Society Museum); (d) 1944 Am 2 242 (presented by Mrs H. Beasley); (e) 1937.6-17.1; (f) 1921.10-14.99 (acquired from the Yorkshire Philosophical Society Museum).
72. (a) 1878.11-1.625 (from the collection of the antiquary Sir Samuel Rush Meyrick and presented by Lieutenant-General Augustus Meyrick); (b) NN; (c) 1921.10-14.95 (acquired from the Yorkshire Philosophical Society Museum); (d) Q78 Am 40; (e) 1931.12.
73. Riksarkivet, Stockholm.
74. Museum of Art, Rhode Island School of Design, gift of Mr Robert Winthrop.
75. Thomas Gilcrease Institute of American History and Art, Tulsa.
76. (a) 1928.10-12.5 (presented by C. A. Morell Miller); (b) 1921.10-4.192 (presented by E. Renouf); (c) on loan from Stonyhurst College; (d) 1921.10-14.107 (acquired from the Yorkshire Philosophical Society Museum); Christy collection (e) D.c.80; (f) D.c. 44.
77. Christy collection D.b.2, 28, D.c.43.
78. 1944 Am 2 208 (acquired by H. Beasley from the Church Missionary Society in 1932 and presented by Mrs H. Beasley).
80. Sloane collection Sl 573; 1944 Am 2

253 (acquired by H. Beasley from the Royal Artillery Museum, Woolwich, and presented by Mrs H. Beasley); 1949 Am 22 129.
81. 1954 W Am 5 1183 (presented by the Trustees of the Wellcome Museum).
82. Christy collection St. 781.
83. Photograph by Charles A. Zimmerman, St Paul. Blackmore collection: B/2944.
84. British Library Board.
85. National Gallery of Canada, Ottawa.
86. British Library Board.
87. Q78 Am 39; 1921.10-14.103 (acquired from the Yorkshire Philosophical Society Museum); 1949 Am 22 143 (from the collection of the Earl of Home, Bothwell Castle); 1878. 11-1.627 (from the collection of the antiquary Sir Samuel Rush Meyrick, and presented by Lieutenant-General Augustus Meyrick).
88. Royal Ontario Museum, Toronto.
89. On loan from Stonyhurst College.
90. 1949 Am 22 146; 1949 Am 22 148; NN; Christy collection 5486; on loan from Stonyhurst College.
91. National Gallery of Canada, Ottawa (gift of the Duke of Westminster).
92. British Library Board.
93. +6993 (acquired from 'Pickering' and presented to the Christy collection by Sir A. W. Franks); 1944 Am 2 214 (acquired by H. Beasley from the Royal Artillery Museum, Woolwich, and presented by Mrs H. Beasley).
94. Sir John Soane's Museum, London.
95. British Museum (Department of Coins and Medals).
96. Museum of the City of New York.
97. Rochester Museum and Science Center.
98. Christy collection 2596, +5167, +3579, 2586; 1944 Am 2 203 (from the collection of Sir George Simpson, presented by Mrs H. Beasley).
99. 1921.10-14.88 (acquired from the Yorkshire Philosophical Society Museum).
100. On loan from Stonyhurst College.

Further reading

BRASSER, TED J. 'A Basketful of Indian Culture Change'. *National Museum of Man Mercury Series, Canadian Ethnology Service Paper No. 22*. Ottawa, 1975.

BRASSER, TED *'Bo'jou, Neejee!' Profiles of Canadian Indian Art,* Ottawa, 1976.

DENSMORE, FRANCES 'Chippewa Customs', *Bureau of American Ethnology Bulletin 86*. Washington D.C., 1929.

FLINT IINSTITUTE OF ARTS *The Art of the Great Lakes Indians*. Flint, 1973.

ORCHARD, WILLIAM C. 'The Technique of Porcupine-quill Decoration among the North American Indians', *Contributions from the Museum of the American Indian Heye Foundation 4(1)*. New York, 1916.

ORCHARD, WILLIAM C. 'Beads and Beadwork of the American Indians', *Contributions from the Museum of the American Indian Heye Foundation 11*. New York, 1929.

RITZENTHALER, ROBERT 'Iroquois False-Face Masks', *Milwaukee Public Museum Publications in Primitive Art 3*. Milwaukee, 1969.

ROGERS, EDWARD S. 'The Material Culture of the Mistassini, *Anthropological Series 80, National Museum of Canada Bulletin 218*. Ottawa, 1967.

SPECK, FRANK G. *Naskapi: The Savage Hunters of the Labrador Peninsular*. Norman, 1935.

SPECK, FRANK G. 'The Iroquois a Study in Cultural Evolution', *Cranbrook Institute of Science Bulletin No. 23*. Bloomfield Hills, 1945.

STURTEVANT, WILLIAM C. (General Editor) *Handbook of North American Indians,* Vol. 15, Northeast, Vol. 6 Subarctic. Washington D.C., 1978 and 1981.

TRIGGER, BRUCE G. *The Huron: Farmers of the North*. New York, 1969.

TURNER, LUCIEN M. 'Ethnology of the Ungava District', *Eleventh Annual Report of the Bureau of Ethnology 1889-'90*. Washington, 1894.

WHITEHEAD, RUTH HOLMES *Elitekey. Micmac Material Culture from 1600 A.D. to the Present*. Halifax, 1980.

The quotes at the beginning of sections are from the following sources:

CARVER, J. *Travels through the Interior Parts of North America in the Years 1766, 1767 and and 1768*. London, 1779.

CHAMPLAIN, SAMUEL DE *The Works of Samuel de Champlain,* vol. 3, H. P. Biggar (ed.). Toronto, 1929.

HERIOT, GEORGE *Travels through the Canadas*. London, 1807.

ISHAM, JAMES 'James Isham's Observations on Hudsons Bay, 1743', E. E. Rich (ed.), *The Hudson's Bay Record Society,* vol. 12. London, 1949.

MORGAN, LEWIS H. *League of the Ho-de'-no-sau-nee, or Iroquois*. Rochester, 1851.

ORCHARD, WILLIAM C. 'Beads and Beadwork of the American Indians', *op. cit.*

TWAIN, MARK *The complete short stories of Mark Twain,* Charles Neider (ed.). New York, 1957.